THRIFTY LIVING MAKEOVER

Mastering Frugality in 30 Days

Ray White

Table of Contents

INTRODUCTION

Welcome to the transformative journey of "Thrifty Living Makeover: Mastering Frugality in 30 Days." In a world where expenses seem to constantly rise, and financial worries linger, this guide is your beacon of light. Over the next month, you'll embark on a fulfilling adventure that will reshape your perspective on money and empower you with the skills to lead a frugal and fulfilling life.

In this fast-paced modern society, the concept of thriftiness has often taken a back seat. The allure of convenience and indulgence has overshadowed the satisfaction that comes from smart financial choices. However, this book is here to rekindle that age-old wisdom of spending thoughtfully and living purposefully.

Through a carefully crafted 30-day plan, you'll learn how to reevaluate your spending habits, distinguish between needs and wants, and harness the power of budgeting. Each day presents a new insight, a fresh perspective, and a practical exercise to help you develop the habits of a frugal lifestyle. From grocery shopping tricks and DIY home solutions to decluttering your space and exploring cost-effective entertainment, you'll gradually embrace a more intentional way of living.

The "Thrifty Living Makeover" isn't just about pinching pennies; it's about regaining control over your finances and channeling your resources toward what truly matters. As you immerse yourself in this journey, you'll discover that frugality doesn't mean deprivation—it means making choices that align with your goals and values.

Get ready to embark on a month-long adventure that will not only revolutionize your relationship with money but also lead you to a more rewarding and mindful life. Let the "Thrifty Living Makeover" guide you toward mastering frugality and embracing the abundance that comes with it.

CHAPTER ONE

Mindful Spending: Foundations of Frugality

Welcome to the first step of your transformative journey toward mastering frugality. In this chapter, we delve into the profound concept of mindful spending—a cornerstone of achieving financial freedom and leading a purposeful life. By understanding the psychological aspects of consumerism, discerning the distinction between needs and wants, and practicing practical exercises, you'll lay a strong foundation for your frugal journey ahead.

The Psychological Landscape of Consumerism

Consumerism—the modern pursuit of material possessions and the constant need for more—has become deeply ingrained in our culture. We are bombarded daily with advertisements that promise happiness through acquisition. However, this unending cycle of buying can lead to a feeling of emptiness and perpetuate financial stress.

Mindful spending encourages us to step off this treadmill and reevaluate our relationship with material possessions. It prompts us to examine our motivations behind purchases and to make choices that align with our values and long-term goals. By breaking free from impulsive buying, we regain control over our finances and find contentment in what we have.

Distinguishing Needs from Wants

Before we can adopt mindful spending habits, we need to clarify the distinction between our genuine needs and our fleeting wants. Needs are the essential requirements for survival and well-being—food, shelter, clothing, and healthcare. Wants, on the other hand, are desires that often arise from societal pressures, trends, or the urge to keep up with others.

One of the first exercises on this frugal journey is to identify your needs and wants. Take a moment to reflect on your recent purchases and categorize them accordingly. Were they motivated by necessity, or were they driven by momentary impulses? Understanding this difference empowers you to make conscious decisions that contribute to your financial health.

The Power of Intentional Spending

Mindful spending is all about intentionality. It's about approaching every purchase with a clear purpose and a conscious evaluation of its impact on your overall well-being. Before making a purchase, ask yourself a few questions:

1. Do I really need this item? Consider whether the purchase aligns with your needs or if it's driven by an immediate desire.

2. What value will this item add to my life? Think about how the item will improve your daily life or contribute to your long-term goals.

3. Can I afford it without compromising my financial goals? Evaluate whether the purchase fits within your budget and won't hinder your progress toward financial freedom.

4. Is there a more frugal alternative? Explore whether there are more cost-effective options that still fulfill your needs or desires.

5. Will this purchase contribute to clutter or fulfillment? Consider whether the item will enhance your life or potentially add to unnecessary clutter.

Practical Exercises: Your Mindful Spending Journey

To help you kick-start your mindful spending journey, let's dive into a couple of practical exercises:

1. Spending Journal:
Start keeping a spending journal. For the next week, jot down every single expense, no matter how small. At the end of the week, review your entries. Categorize each expense as a need or want. Reflect on the patterns you notice. Are there areas where you consistently spend on wants? This exercise will raise your awareness of your spending habits and provide insights into areas where you can practice mindful spending.

2. The 24-Hour Rule:
Before making a non-essential purchase, implement the 24-hour rule. When you feel the urge to buy something on a whim, give yourself 24 hours to think it over. During this time, evaluate whether the purchase aligns with your values and goals. Often, you'll find that the initial excitement fades, leading you to make more intentional choices.

Conclusion: Embrace the Mindful Spending Mindset

As you embark on this frugal journey, remember that mindful spending isn't about deprivation—it's about empowerment. By understanding the psychological aspects of consumerism, discerning between needs and wants, and adopting intentional spending practices, you're laying the groundwork for financial freedom and a life filled with purpose.

In the next chapter, we'll delve into the practical art of creating a budget blueprint—a powerful tool that will guide you toward your financial goals. Get ready to take control of your finances and design the life you've always envisioned.

CHAPTER TWO

Creating a Budget Blueprint: Your Financial Roadmap

Welcome to the heart of your journey toward mastering frugality—creating a budget blueprint that will serve as your financial roadmap. In this chapter, we will dive deep into the nitty-gritty of budgeting, guiding you through the process of crafting a comprehensive budget that aligns with your income, aspirations, and dreams. By understanding budget categories, tracking your expenses, setting achievable financial targets, and learning to adapt as circumstances change, you will lay the foundation for a secure and fulfilling financial future.

The Essence of Budgeting

At its core, budgeting is a conscious and systematic approach to managing your money. It's not about restriction; it's about empowerment. A budget empowers you to allocate your resources in a way that reflects your priorities and long-term goals. It's a tool that helps you control your finances rather than letting them control you.

Building Your Budget: Step by Step

Let's walk through the process of creating a budget that suits your unique financial situation:

1. Assess Your Income: Begin by calculating your total monthly income. This includes not only your salary but also any additional sources of income, such as freelancing or rental income.

2. Identify Fixed Expenses: List your fixed expenses—those that remain constant each month, such as rent or mortgage payments, utilities, insurance premiums, and loan payments.

3. Track Variable Expenses: Track your variable expenses, which can fluctuate from month to month. These include groceries, dining out, entertainment, and other discretionary spending.

4. Set Financial Goals: Define your short-term and long-term financial goals. These could range from paying off debt and building an emergency fund to saving for a vacation or a down payment on a home.

5. Allocate Funds: Allocate your income to various budget categories based on their importance and urgency. Prioritize essential expenses and allocate a portion to your financial goals.

6. Monitor and Adjust: Regularly track your spending to ensure you're staying within your budgeted amounts. If you find that you're overspending in certain categories, adjust your budget accordingly.

Budget Categories: Beyond the Basics

Understanding budget categories is crucial for effective financial planning. Here are some categories to consider:

1. Necessities: This includes housing, utilities, transportation, groceries, and insurance.

2. Debt Repayment: Allocate funds to paying off debts, such as credit cards, student loans, and personal loans.

3. Savings and Investments: Set aside money for your emergency fund, retirement accounts, and other investments.

4. Goals and Dreams: Budget for your aspirations, whether it's buying a car, traveling, or purchasing a home.

5. Discretionary Spending: This covers non-essential expenses like entertainment, dining out, and shopping.

Benefits of a Clear Financial Roadmap

A well-structured budget offers numerous benefits beyond just managing your money:

1. Financial Control: A budget empowers you to make informed financial decisions and curbs impulse spending.

2. Goal Achievement: You'll be better positioned to achieve your financial goals, both short-term and long-term.

3. Reduced Stress: Knowing where your money is going reduces financial anxiety and fosters peace of mind.

4. Emergency Preparedness: An emergency fund funded through your budget acts as a safety net during unexpected events.

Adapting to Changing Circumstances

Life is dynamic, and so should be your budget. Be prepared to adjust your budget as circumstances change—whether it's a new job, a growing family, or unexpected expenses. Flexibility ensures that your budget remains relevant and effective.

Conclusion: Your Financial Journey Begins

As you embark on this chapter's teachings, remember that your budget is not a rigid constraint; it's a tool for empowerment and financial growth. By creating a budget blueprint tailored to your income and goals, you're taking a pivotal step toward mastering frugality and securing your financial future. In the next chapter, we'll delve into the art of adopting smart shopping strategies that help you cut costs without sacrificing quality or enjoyment. Get ready to transform your spending habits and unlock a world of financial possibilities.

CHAPTER THREE

Smart Shopping Strategies: Cutting Costs without Sacrifice

Welcome to the world of savvy shopping, where every purchase becomes an opportunity to save and make meaningful choices. In this chapter, we'll explore transformative strategies that go beyond traditional shopping habits. From grocery shopping to clothing and household essentials, we'll delve into the art of cutting costs without compromising quality or enjoyment. Get ready to embrace conscious choices that lead to substantial savings and a more fulfilling frugal lifestyle.

Grocery Shopping Reinvented: Meal Planning, Buying in Bulk, and Coupons

1. Meal Planning Mastery:
Meal planning is a cornerstone of frugal living. By mapping out your meals for the week ahead, you not only save money but also reduce food waste. Create a weekly meal plan, taking stock of items you already have and incorporating them into your recipes. This minimizes the need for last-minute grocery runs and prevents impulse buying.

2. Buying in Bulk for Savings:

Bulk buying is a cost-effective approach for items you frequently use, such as grains, pasta, nuts, and cleaning supplies. Look for bulk bins at grocery stores or consider joining a wholesale club. However, be mindful of storage space and expiration dates to ensure you're truly saving.

3. Unveiling the Power of Coupons:

Coupons, whether digital or traditional, can significantly slash your grocery bill. Collect coupons for items you regularly purchase and plan your meals around discounted products. Combine coupons with store sales for maximum savings. Just be cautious not to buy items solely because you have a coupon—stick to your planned list.

Wise Wardrobe Choices: Dressing Well on a Budget

1. Timeless vs. Trendy:

When it comes to clothing, opt for timeless pieces that can be mixed and matched. These classics transcend trends and provide more value for your money. While it's okay to indulge in trendy items occasionally, invest in quality basics that can form the foundation of your wardrobe.

2. Secondhand Sensibility:

Thrift stores, consignment shops, and online platforms offer a treasure trove of gently used clothing at a fraction of the cost. Embrace the thrill of the hunt and discover unique pieces that align with your personal style. Remember, someone else's pre-loved garment can become your stylish find.

3. DIY and Upcycling:

Get creative with your wardrobe by upcycling old clothing items. Transform jeans into shorts, add patches to jackets, or embellish a plain t-shirt. With a bit of ingenuity and basic sewing skills, you can breathe new life into your existing wardrobe without spending a dime.

Practical Home Economics: From Essentials to Luxuries

1. Household Essentials for Less:

Household items like cleaning supplies, toiletries, and paper products can quickly add up. Consider purchasing these in bulk or opting for store brands, which often offer comparable quality at a lower cost. Look for sales and deals, and don't underestimate the power of DIY alternatives for cleaning solutions.

2. Prioritizing Value Over Brand:

When shopping for electronics, appliances, or home goods, prioritize value and functionality over brand names. Research products that meet your needs and read reviews to ensure quality. You'll find that there are many alternatives that offer the same features without the hefty price tag.

3. Finding Joy in Minimalism:

As you navigate through your shopping journey, embrace the principles of minimalism. Prioritize experiences and quality over material possessions. Often, the satisfaction derived from mindful consumption far surpasses the fleeting thrill of impulse buying.

Conclusion: Elevating Your Shopping Game

As you've immersed yourself in the world of smart shopping strategies, you've gained a powerful set of tools for cutting costs without sacrifice. Whether it's through meal planning, bulk buying, coupon clipping, secondhand shopping, or conscious home economics, each choice you make contributes to your financial well-being and a more intentional lifestyle.

In the next chapter, we'll explore the transformative impact of frugalizing your lifestyle. From decluttering your space to embracing minimalism, get ready to experience the freedom and contentment that come from living with intention. Your journey to mastering frugality continues, unlocking new dimensions of fulfillment along the way.

CHAPTER FOUR

Frugalizing Your Lifestyle: Simple Living for Abundant Joy

Welcome to the realm of intentional living—a place where frugality is not a constraint, but a gateway to profound contentment and abundance. In this chapter, we journey into the heart of simple living, exploring how embracing frugality can be a deliberate choice that leads to increased joy and fulfillment. From decluttering and minimalism to the art of repurposing and upcycling, you're about to discover the transformative power of owning less and experiencing life more deeply.

The Essence of Simple Living

At its core, simple living is about prioritizing experiences and values over material possessions. It's the conscious decision to detach from the consumerist treadmill and focus on what truly matters. By embracing frugality, you open the door to a world where less clutter leads to more freedom, and where mindful choices amplify the richness of your existence.

Decluttering: The Liberation of Letting Go

1. The Joy of Less:
Clutter in our surroundings often mirrors the chaos within us. Begin your journey to simple living by decluttering your space. One room at a time, assess your belongings and ask yourself: Does this item bring me joy or serve a purpose? If not, it's time to let it go. Embrace the newfound space and clarity that decluttering offers.

2. The 80/20 Rule:
The Pareto Principle, also known as the 80/20 rule, applies to possessions too. We tend to use only about 20% of our belongings regularly. Identify these essentials and consider parting with the rest. This practice not only reduces clutter but also streamlines your daily life.

Minimalism: Finding Abundance in Less

1. The Beauty of Minimalist Aesthetics:
Minimalism is more than just aesthetics; it's a way of life. Embrace clean lines, open spaces, and purposeful design. Surrounding yourself with fewer, carefully chosen items fosters an environment of tranquility and focus.

2. The Emotional Impact of Possessions:
Minimalism encourages you to forge a deeper connection with your possessions. Each item you own gains significance, as it's chosen with intention rather than accumulated indiscriminately. This mindset shift elevates the emotional value of your belongings.

Repurposing and Upcycling: A Creative Approach to Consumption

1. A Second Life for Items:
Instead of discarding items that seem no longer useful, explore creative ways to repurpose them. Old clothing can become stylish accessories, glass jars can transform into candle holders, and wooden pallets can become functional furniture. Repurposing not only reduces waste but also ignites your creativity.

2. The Art of Upcycling:
Upcycling takes repurposing a step further by turning old or discarded items into something of higher value. Upcycling projects can range from turning worn-out jeans into fashionable bags to transforming broken furniture into unique pieces that showcase your personality.

DIY Projects: Unleashing Your Inner Creative Genius

1. DIY Home Solutions:
Tackle household projects with a do-it-yourself attitude. From crafting homemade cleaning solutions to revamping your living space, DIY projects not only save money but also infuse your surroundings with a personalized touch.

2. Handmade Gifts and Treasures:
Consider gifting handmade creations to loved ones. Whether it's a hand-painted mug, a knitted scarf, or a carefully curated recipe book, these thoughtful gifts carry a unique charm that store-bought items simply can't replicate.

Conclusion: Living the Abundant Frugal Life

As you embark on your journey to frugalizing your lifestyle, remember that simple living is a profound choice that leads to abundant joy. By decluttering, embracing minimalism, repurposing, and indulging in DIY projects, you're tapping into the wellspring of creativity and fulfillment that comes from intentional living.

In the next chapter, we'll explore the world of entertainment on a budget, uncovering the myriad ways to create meaningful experiences without overspending. Get ready to enrich your life with memorable moments and deepen your connection to what truly matters. Your journey toward mastering frugality continues, unlocking new horizons of contentment and discovery.

CHAPTER FIVE

Entertainment on a Budget: Cultivating Meaningful Experiences

Welcome to the realm of budget-friendly entertainment, where joy and connection flourish without putting a strain on your wallet. In this chapter, we'll unveil the art of creating memorable experiences that enrich your life and nurture your relationships, all while embracing the frugal lifestyle. From free community events and outdoor adventures to the joy of frugal hobbies and the mindfulness of the present moment, get ready to discover a world of meaningful entertainment that aligns with your values and aspirations.

The Power of Meaningful Experiences

Entertainment doesn't have to be synonymous with extravagant spending. Meaningful experiences stem from genuine connections, inner fulfillment, and shared moments that resonate deeply. By shifting the focus from material consumption to enriching experiences, you'll find that joy can be found in the simplest of pleasures.

Exploring Free and Community Events

1. Local Cultural Offerings:
Communities often host free or low-cost cultural events, such as art exhibitions, music festivals, and theater performances. These events not only provide entertainment but also offer opportunities to connect with local artists and fellow attendees.

2. Public Lectures and Workshops:
Many libraries, universities, and cultural centers host public lectures, workshops, and discussions on a wide range of topics. Engaging in these events not only expands your knowledge but also introduces you to like-minded individuals.

3. Outdoor Concerts and Movies:
During warmer months, keep an eye out for outdoor concerts and movie screenings in parks and public spaces. Pack a picnic, gather your friends or family, and enjoy entertainment under the open sky.

Embracing the Great Outdoors

1. Nature Walks and Hikes:
Reconnect with nature by exploring local trails, parks, and nature reserves. Nature walks and hikes

offer not only physical activity but also a chance to disconnect from the digital world and find solace in natural beauty.

2. Picnics and Outdoor Gatherings:
Host picnics or outdoor potlucks with friends and family. The simple act of sharing a meal in a park can create cherished memories and foster a sense of togetherness.

3. Stargazing and Nighttime Adventures:
Witness the magic of the night sky by stargazing in areas with minimal light pollution. Set up a cozy spot, bring blankets, and marvel at the wonders of the universe.

The Joy of Frugal Hobbies

1. Gardening and Green Spaces:
Tending to a garden, whether it's a windowsill herb garden or a backyard oasis, is not only therapeutic but also rewarding. Cultivating plants and flowers connects you to the cycles of nature and provides a sense of accomplishment.

2. Creative Arts and Crafts:
Engage in artistic hobbies like painting, drawing, knitting, or crafting. These activities allow you to

express your creativity and produce unique pieces that reflect your personality.

3. Cooking and Culinary Adventures:
Experiment with cooking new recipes or hosting potluck dinners with friends. Sharing meals you've prepared not only showcases your culinary skills but also strengthens social bonds.

Mindfulness and Meaning in the Moment

1. Meditation and Mindful Practices:
Engage in mindfulness practices that ground you in the present moment. Meditation, deep breathing, and yoga cultivate inner peace and promote overall well-being.

2. Journaling and Reflection:
Document your thoughts, experiences, and gratitude in a journal. Regular reflection enhances self-awareness and fosters a sense of gratitude for the simple joys in life.

3. Volunteering and Giving Back:
Engage in volunteer opportunities that align with your values. Contributing to your community or a cause you're passionate about creates a sense of purpose and enriches your life.

Conclusion: Nurturing Joy Through Connection

As you embark on the journey of cultivating meaningful experiences on a budget, remember that true joy emerges from genuine connections and mindful moments. By exploring free community events, embracing the outdoors, pursuing frugal hobbies, and engaging in mindful practices, you're opening the door to a world of contentment and enrichment.

In the next chapter, we'll delve into the importance of maintaining financial sustainability while also planning for the future. Get ready to uncover the strategies that will empower you to navigate unexpected expenses and achieve lasting financial resilience. Your quest to master frugality continues, leading you toward a life of abundance and purpose.